The Spice Girls

Julia Holt

Published in association with The Basic Skills Agency

Hodder & Stoughton

A MEMBER OF THE HODDER HEADLINE GROUP

Acknowledgements

Photos: p. iv © All Action/John Mather, pp. 6, 10, 13, 16 and 19 © Famous/Rob Howard.
Cover photo: © Famous/Rob Howard.

The author and the publishers would like to thank Patrick Walters for his assistance in researching the material for this book.

This is an unofficial biography.

Orders: please contact Bookpoint Ltd, 39 Milton Park, Abingdon, Oxon OX14 4TD. Telephone: (44) 01235 400414, Fax: (44) 01235 400454. Lines are open from 9.00–6.00, Monday to Saturday, with a 24 hour message answering service. Email address: orders@bookpoint.co.uk

British Library Cataloguing in Publication Data
A catalogue record for this title is available from The British Library

ISBN 0 340 71151 5

First published 1998

Impression number 10 9 8 7 6 5 4 3 2
Year 2002 2001 2000 1999 1998

Typeset by Fakenham Photosetting Ltd, Fakenham, Norfolk.
Printed in Great Britain for Hodder & Stoughton Educational, a division of Hodder Headline Plc, 338 Euston Road, London NW1 3BH by Page Bros Ltd, Norwich.

Contents

1 Early Wannabees

Before July 1996
the Spice Girls were wannabees.
Now they are famous
all over the world.

They have had more success
than any British girl band ever.

Their dream has come true.
Not by magic but by hard work.

On 4 March 1994
400 hopeful girls
had one minute each
to sing and dance.

They had all seen an advert
in *The Stage* newspaper.
It said:
'Wannabe starlets. RU 18–34
with the ability to sing/dance?'

Chris Herbert put the advert
in the paper.
It was his idea to form a girl band
and call them 'Touch'.

Chris saw all 400 girls and he chose:
Mel B, Mel C, Victoria and Michelle.

He did not see Geri
because she was working that day.
Geri begged Chris to give her a try.
She looked older than the others,
so Chris asked her age.
Geri's reply was a classic.
She said:
'I'm as old as you want me to be.'
She was in.

One month later,
the five girls got down to work.

They spent the first week
trying to sing and dance together.
But it was not a big success.
They were told to go home
and think hard –
was this really what they wanted to do?

All five girls said 'Yes',
so Chris rented a house for them to live in.
They had to live very simply
because they had no wages.
They were only given a little pocket money.

Every day they went to a studio
to work on their singing and dancing.
Geri had to work the hardest
because she wasn't as good as the others.
She put in extra hours and often said:
'Time is running out.
This is my last chance
and I'm going to make it.'

Sadly, Michelle did not fit in.
She didn't want to do
what the others wanted to do.
They didn't have to dump her.
She left to look after her sick mother
and then to go to university.
Emma was chosen to take her place.

Now the girls started to work together
as a team.

2 Girl Power!

Mel B and Geri both wanted to be boss.
They had lots of fights
but Mel C always sorted them out.
Victoria looked after the money
and Emma cheered everybody up.

The next two years flew by.
The girls wrote over 30 songs.
They changed their name
from 'Touch' to 'The Spice Girls'.
At night,
they did a song and dance act
in front of the bedroom mirror.

At the weekends,
Victoria and Emma went home,
Mel C watched football,
and Mel B and Geri went clubbing.

They also chose a style for the band.
They didn't want to look boring,
like other teen bands before.
So they chose to be themselves.

Sporty Spice, Baby Spice,
Posh Spice, Scary Spice
and Ginger Spice.

Then the Spice Girls had problems
with their manager, Chris.

He wanted them all to dress the same,
and sing other people's songs.
But they wanted to be in control.

They wanted a new manager,
someone who let them do their own thing.

In April 1995,
they signed with Simon Fuller.
He is also the manager of Annie Lennox.
Simon got them a £2 million contract
with Virgin Records.
Girl Power was on the way!

Melanie Brown – Scary Spice

3 Scary Spice

Name: Melanie Brown

Birthday: 29 May 1975

Height: 5 feet 5 inches

Eyes: Brown

Body art: Pierced tongue and a tattoo
on her belly
It says 'Spirit, Heart and Mind'
in Japanese.

From: Leeds

Likes: Fish and chips

Hates: Liars and salads

Mum: Andrea – she is a cleaner

Dad: Martin – he works shifts in a factory
and rides a bike to work.

Sister: Danielle – aged 16

Mel B is loud and proud.
She is also very honest.

Her mum says:
'She has always been the sort of girl
who would only do what she wanted.'

Mel went to college
to study singing, dancing and drumming.

Aged 17,
she was paid £3.00 an hour
for dancing in a bikini in a nightclub.
Then she won a car
and a trip to Disneyland
in a local beauty contest.

She went on to have bit parts
in Coronation Street
and Emmerdale.

Then she moved to London.
She got a job skating in a show
called 'Starlight Express'.

But a few months after,
she was chosen as a Spice Girl.

4 Sporty Spice

Name: Melanie Chisholm

Birthday: 12 January 1976

Height: 5 feet 6 inches

Eyes: Hazel

Body art: Celtic tattoo round her right arm
               and a pierced nose.

From: Widnes near Liverpool

Likes: Football

Hates: Smoking

Mum: Joan – she is a secretary,
               and she sings in clubs.

Step-dad: Den – he was in a band
               called 'The Addicts' in the 1960s.

Dad: Alan – he is a manager of
               a coach hire firm.
               He and Joan split up
               when Mel C was little.
               But Mel is still in touch with him.

Brother: Paul – aged 16

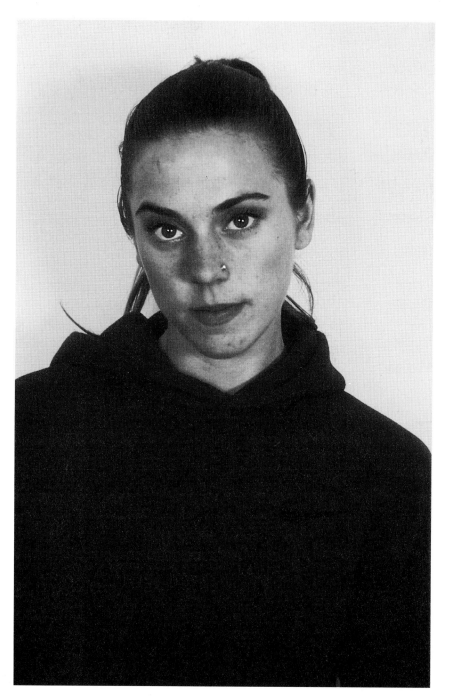

Melanie Chisholm – Sporty Spice

Everyone knows Mel C is mad about football.
But her first love is ballet.
When she was little,
she took extra ballet lessons on Saturdays.
She gets her singing talent
from her mum and step-dad.

Mel C is shy,
but she always wanted to perform.
She was in all the school plays.

Her friends remember her
as a good actress,
but an even better singer.

After she left school,
she moved to Kent.
She went to a dance school
to study ballet and jazz dance.
To make ends meet,
she worked in a chip shop.

Mel C tried to get work
in many musical shows.

She was down to the last five
for a part in 'Cats',
when she was chosen to be a Spice Girl.

5 Posh Spice

Name: Victoria Adams

Birthday: 7 March 1975

Height: 5 feet 6 inches

Eyes: Brown

Body art: Pierced ears,
and a diamond in her fingernail.

From: Hertfordshire

Likes: Shopping

Hates: Japanese food

Mum: Jackie – she runs a big electrical firm
with Victoria's dad.

Dad: Tony – he was in a 1960s band
called 'The Sonics'.

Sister: Louise, aged 19

Brother: Christian, aged 17

Fiancé David Beckham of
Manchester United and England.

Victoria Adams – Posh Spice

Victoria is cool and classy,
and she always was.
She lived with her parents
in a big old house in a village
in Hertfordshire.

They had a swimming pool,
and her dad took her to school
in his Rolls Royce.

Her mum says:
'All Victoria ever wanted to do
was dance.'

At 16,
she went to drama school
for three years.
Then she joined a small musical company
on tour.

After that, she joined a band,
but left them to be a Spice Girl.

In January 1998,
she got engaged to David Beckham,
the footballer.

6 Baby Spice

Name: Emma Bunton

Birthday: 21 January 1976

Height: 5 feet 2 inches

Eyes: Blue

Body art: None

From: North London

Likes: Sweets and chocolate

Hates: Bad doughnuts

Mum: Pauline – she runs a karate club.

Dad: Trevor – he is a milkman,
and he doesn't live with Pauline.

Brother: Paul, aged 16

Emma Bunton – Baby Spice

Emma was always going to be a star.

From the age of five,
she was a model for Mothercare.
She went abroad for photo-shoots
every year until she was twelve.

Her mum saved all Emma's wages
to pay for Emma to go to drama school
when she was 16.

Emma loves singing and dancing,
but she is not all sugar and spice.

She has a blue belt in karate.

At drama school,
she tried to get work in TV.
She wanted the part of Bianca
in EastEnders.
But then,
along came the job with the Spice Girls,
and Emma left drama school to join them.

7 Ginger Spice

Name: Geri Halliwell

Birthday: 6 August 1972

Height: 5 feet 2 inches

Eyes: Blue

Body art: Pierced ears and belly button.
A tattoo of a jaguar on her arm,
and one on her back,
and a sundial on her shoulder.

From: Watford

Likes: Strong women

Hates: Men who smell

Mum: Anna-Maria – she is Spanish.

Dad: Lawrence – he was a car-dealer.
(That's why Geri got a jaguar tattoo!)
He and Anna-Maria split up
when Geri was little,
and he died of a heart attack in 1993.

Brother: Max

Geri Halliwell – Ginger Spice

Geri is a strong woman,
and she was a strong little girl.
Her mum worked,
so Geri had to get herself off to
school everyday.

She did not have singing and dancing lessons.
But she still wanted to be in showbiz.

Geri has always looked after her body.
At one point,
she was a keep-fit teacher.

Geri was first famous in Turkey.
She was the girl who showed the prizes
on a TV quiz show.

Then she got a job
checking videos for swear words.
She was also a model,
and she tried to be a Page Three Girl.
She gave up nude modelling
to be a Spice Girl.

8 Record Breakers

Virgin Records called a meeting
to sign the girls.
They couldn't make it
but they sent five blow-up dolls
to take their places.

Virgin said
they were going to make the Spice Girls
the world's top pop band.

Most new bands have to work their way up
by doing lots of little shows in small towns.
Not the Spice Girls!
They had the backing of a big record company.
Their first single 'Wannabe'
came out in July 1996.
It went to the No 1 spot
and stayed there for eight weeks.

'Wannabe' also went to No 1
in 31 other countries.
It is Virgin's biggest selling single
in 13 years.

The Spice Girls are the first girl band
to have their first single go to No 1.
This gives them a place
in the Guinness Book of Records.

For the rest of 1996
the girls' feet never touched the ground.
They did shows in 37 countries
scaring and shocking people
wherever they went.

Geri and Mel B
hand-cuffed a night club manager to a tree.
He wanted to shut his club at midnight
but they wanted to party.
They had food fights.
They ran wild in the studio of
Top of the Pops.
They scared the other pop stars.
Geri said:
'We're in charge all the way.'

The next two Spice Girls singles
went to No 1.
'Say You'll Be There'
went platinum after only five days.
600,000 copies were sold in a week.

The video for the single
showed the girls doing karate in the desert.

'2 Become 1'
was No 1 over Christmas of 1996.
The Spice Girls held the single back for
a week to let the Dunblane single
have a chance to be No 1.

When they made the video
for '2 Become 1'
the Spice Girls stopped the traffic
in New York for an hour.
Mel C and Victoria were lifted up onto
a bridge and everyone stopped to look.

Their first three singles
were from their first album, 'Spice'.
It came out on 4 November 1996.
The girls helped to write all of the
ten songs on it.
So far the album has sold 10 million copies.

The Spice Girls arrived at the top.
They switched on the Christmas lights
in London.
They sang on the National Lottery show
and they won three of the Smash Hits awards.

Their plan for 1997
was to have a hit in America.
First they took a short holiday.
Emma played bingo with her mum in Barbados.
Then the Spice Girls went to the USA.

'Wannabe' went into the US charts at No 11.
This was the highest ever entry
by a British band.
It went up to No 1
and stayed there for four weeks.

The girls made an advert for Pepsi.
They were paid $1 million
for one day's work.
Then they flew home.

At the Brit Awards in February 1997
they won Best Single
and Best Video.
Geri wore her famous Union Jack mini dress.
Her boobs popped out twice,
but she said:
'This is the best night of our lives.
So I don't care what happens.'

'Mama' was the fourth single
from the album 'Spice'.
It went to No 1 as well,
making record history.
The Spice Girls are the first band ever
to have four No 1 hits
with their first four singles.

'Mama' came out on Mother's Day.
They made it to thank their mums.
Emma says:
'My mum is my No 1.
She's always there for me.'

The Spice Girls made a spoof video
for Comic Relief, with French and Saunders.
They also gave all their profits
from 'Mama' to Comic Relief.

The Spice Girls were in at the start of
Channel 5. They were all dressed in rubber
in the colours of Channel 5.

9 The Future

In April 1997 the Spice Girls video came out
and so did the book, 'Girl Power'.
It was on sale all over the world
in 20 different languages.

They have made a second album, 'Spiceworld'.
'Spiceworld' has sold
over nine million copies worldwide.

The Spice Girls have also made a movie.
It is called 'Spiceworld – the Movie'.
Jennifer Saunders wrote it,
and many stars are in it.
It tells the story of a week
in the crazy lives of the Spice Girls.

Many critics said that the Spice Girls
would only last one or two years.
But the second album
and the film
have done much better
than the critics said they would.

However, in June 1998,
Geri – Ginger Spice – said that
she was leaving the Spice Girls.
She said that this was because of
differences with the other girls.

Sporty, Scary, Baby and Posh
have said that they will carry on
without Ginger Spice.

But will this prove to be
the end of the Spice Girls?
Or will Girl Power
and the Spice Girls
be around for a while yet?